DEAR READER,

Are you under eighteen years old? Then this book is for you and about you! Although, I would encourage you to lend it, read it aloud to, or stick it under the nose of anybody within your reach. Because this book is about YOUR rights, and unless we all know about them – adults, children, rich, poor, big and small – unless we share them, treasure them and stand up for them, they can vanish. This would be a terrible backward step, and something very special, which started in 1923 with a lady called Eglantyne Jebb, would be lost. And once lost, it will be much harder to get back.

"What is this dotty author talking about?"

Yes, I heard your thoughts – but if you want to know what I'm talking about you'll just have to read the incredible stories in this book!

Go on, I only wrote it so you would.
Hooray for you – but only if you do!

Marcia

Impossible!

You'd better believe it guys!

Knowledge is power!

"If children are given an opportunity, they for sure can contribute to making this world a better place."
Thandiwe Chama

**For all children everywhere
– including Cecily, Mathilda and Flora!**

First published 2019 by Walker Books Ltd,
87 Vauxhall Walk, London SE11 5HJ

Paperback edition published 2020

2 4 6 8 10 9 7 5 3 1

Text and illustrations © 2019 Marcia Williams

Cover and title page hand lettering by Gillian Hibbs

The right of Marcia Williams to be identified as author/illustrator of this work has been asserted by her in accordance with the Copyright, Designs and Patents Act 1988

This book has been typeset in Minion

Printed in China

British Cataloguing in Publication Data is available

ISBN 978-1-4063-8410-9 (Hardback)

ISBN 978-1-4063-9029-2 (Paperback)

www.walker.co.uk

MARCIA WILLIAMS

CHILDREN who CHANGED THE WORLD

WE
ARE THE
FUTURE!

WALKER BOOKS
AND SUBSIDIARIES
LONDON · BOSTON · SYDNEY · AUCKLAND

Are all the rights in this book?

Yes, but not every right has its own page!

Some of these activists must be adults by now.

YOUR RIGHTS!

If you shut your eyes and count to sixty – slowly – a minute will have gone by. In that minute approximately two hundred and fifty babies will have been born. This means that somewhere in the world, approximately two hundred and forty-nine babies were born at the very same minute as you! These babies are your brothers and sisters in childhood. You may never meet any of them, but they all have the same right as you – the right to a safe and happy childhood.

You may be reading this in a lovely school or comfortable home, but not all children have such a good start. Some are born in a country at war; others to parents too poor to care for them; others are discriminated against because of disability, religion or race.

To make sure all children, whoever they are and wherever they live, have the support and protection they deserve, a lady called Eglantyne Jebb wrote the first rights for children in 1923. These rights grew into the 54 articles of the Convention on the Rights of the Child. World leaders agreed on these in 1989 and now 196 countries follow them. They give you the right to live in safety, to be listened to and to enjoy your childhood.

The amazing and true stories in this book are about the children who have stood up for these rights – they are activists. They fight for their rights, your rights and every child's rights!

But they were kids when they took up the fight!

They are awesome!

I can't wait to turn the page...

MOHAMAD AL JOUNDE

(BORN 2001, SYRIA)

It doesn't matter where you live or who you are: if you are under eighteen, the Rights of the Child were written for you! But they need to be protected. When Mohamad Al Jounde fled war in his country and became a refugee, he suddenly lost some of the rights he had once enjoyed. He is not the only one to have been denied his rights – many children don't know about their rights or don't have the power to fight for them. When Mohamad realized this, he decided to stand up for every child's rights.

MOHAMAD was born in Syria, where he lived with his family for ten happy years. He had a loving home, friends and a good school, and enjoyed sport and music. Then in 2011 the Syrian Revolution started and Mohamad's life changed.

Happy birthday!

The bombs are getting closer.

What about my toys?

Leave them, we must hurry.

Life in Syria became increasingly dangerous. Eventually Mohamad's family were forced to leave everything and flee to Lebanon.

What will I do without you, Papa?

You'll take photographs – I have left my camera on your bed.

In Lebanon life was hard, and Mohamad's father left to seek work in Sweden. As a refugee, Mohamad was unable to go to school.

Kids who stand up for other kids are very brave.

Child activists are world changers!

Mohamad lost so much so quickly.

Instead, Mohamad learnt photography and made friends with children in the refugee camp.

Mohamad was amazed at how positive the refugee children were. He was inspired to help them.

The children had no school, so Mohamad began teaching them Maths and English. He used his photography to help them create happy memories.

Mohamad was just twelve when he persuaded his family and other volunteers to create a tent school in the camp.

Eventually, they managed to open a permanent school and over 200 children joined! It was a place to learn, to tell their stories, make friends and develop hope. Mohamad saw the children as his family and Syria's future. He was determined to see that they did not become a lost generation, but had a fair chance at life. In 2017 Mohamad won the International Children's Peace Prize for his amazing efforts in making sure that every child has their rights respected and upheld, no matter where they are.

"I'll try to be your voice and your hope so that you can dream big and enjoy life."

FRANCIA SIMON

(BORN 1994, DOMINICAN REPUBLIC)

You may not realize just how important your name is. When it's registered with your country's government, it gives you the right to education, healthcare and more. Francia Simon discovered this when she was stopped from going to school because her parents, who were refugees, hadn't registered her for a birth certificate. Other children end up in a similar situation because their parents don't have the right documents themselves, or don't understand their importance. So Francia dedicated herself to helping children gain their right to a name and identity.

FRANCIA grew up in a very poor community in the Dominican Republic. Her family, and most of her neighbours, were refugees from Haiti. Many had arrived without official papers.

Francia worked hard at primary school, but then she found she didn't have the right registration documents to go on to secondary school.

Francia's family had arrived from Haiti without official papers. But Francia wanted an education, so she applied for a birth certificate.

I love this right!

It's just about a tiny slip of paper.

Yes, but one that brings huge benefits.

It was not easy and Francia struggled. But she would not give up, because a birth certificate was her passport to secondary school!

Finally, Francia succeeded! Now she had her papers, but many other children did not – so she decided to help them.

The authorities often turned the young people away, but Francia always insisted that every child had the right to registration papers.

Whenever a judge issued a birth certificate Francia would check it. If there were any mistakes she would return it to be corrected!

As well as helping children apply for their papers, Francia organized sports, games and special events for those who had fled Haiti as refugees. But her main passion was helping children to gain their documents. In 2010, Francia won the International Children's Peace Prize for her campaign to give children their right to a name, a country and the chance of a more hopeful future.

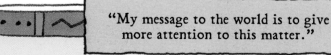
"My message to the world is to give more attention to this matter."

EMILY-ANNE RIGAL

(BORN 1994, USA)

We are all different and have different thoughts and opinions. It is your right to say what you think and feel but it is also important to respect the opinions of others – even if you don't like them! It can be difficult to enjoy your right to express yourself if you are being bullied, as Emily-Anne Rigal found out. She saw that by standing up to bullying we help to protect our right to free speech, so she found a way to encourage young people not to be negative about their differences, but to celebrate them.

EMILY-ANNE was very unhappy at her primary school. The other children teased her because of the way she looked and the clothes she wore. Nobody wanted to be her friend.

Look what she's wearing!

Where did you get that hairband?

You're a loser!

You look gross!

Don't sit next to her!

Can I sit with you?

No way!

No way!

Bow away!

Emily-Anne didn't want to change her look, but the bullying made her so unhappy that she eventually left the school.

Hey, love the look.

Let's be friends.

Really?

Really!

At her new school the children greeted Emily-Anne warmly, and she soon had lots of friends who liked her just the way she was.

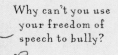

Why can't you use your freedom of speech to bully?

Woof!

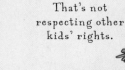

That's not respecting other kids' rights.

I think it's great that we are all different.

As Emily-Anne grew happier she noticed that other children were being bullied – often by young people who felt bad about themselves.

So Emily-Anne launched the YouTube channel WeStopHate, dedicated to ending bullying by encouraging young people to value themselves.

By the time she was sixteen, Emily-Anne's WeStopHate project was reaching young people all over the world. Through posts on YouTube and other social media, she gave both bullies and the bullied a space to share their experiences, discuss their fears and start to feel better about themselves, while encouraging kindness towards others. By bravely telling her own story and through her tireless campaigning, public appearances and writing, Emily-Anne has helped hundreds of young people gain the confidence to enjoy their right to express who they truly are.

"Those who feel good about themselves don't put others down."

MAYRA AVELLAR NEVES

(BORN 1991, BRAZIL)

Every child has the right to be protected from harm. Sadly, many children still suffer from violence, whether from wars, abuse hidden in the home or crime in their neighbourhood. Mayra Avellar Neves was one of these children, living in a community in Brazil that was overrun with dangerous street gangs. Mayra realized that children living in fear were unable to enjoy their other rights, like going to school or playing. So Mayra decided to stand up for their right to be protected from violence.

MAYRA was born into a poor but loving family in a favela, or slum, of Rio de Janeiro. It was a violent area that suffered from endless gang battles. Like many of her friends, Mayra could not safely walk or play in the streets.

Mayra, always stand up against violence.

But that's scary!

Let's just stay here today, it's not safe outside.

What about school?

Mayra's house was pitted with bullet holes and she often had to hide under her bed to avoid stray bullets.

Look, another child lost to violence. I'm scared to walk to school, Mama.

ABERTO, WE WILL MISS YOU

The police would try to break up the gangs, but every year children lost their lives in the battles that followed in the streets.

Poor Mayra, what a scary childhood.

I'd never want to go outside.

Mayra was a shining light in a dark and dangerous place!

When Mayra was eleven the schools in her area were closed because of the violence. Luckily, Mayra gained a place in a school outside the favela. Here Mayra saw a more peaceful way of life – she realized that not all children have their lives interrupted by violence.

Mayra knew that without the same opportunities, many children from the favelas would grow up to be without jobs or in gangs. When she was fifteen, Mayra organized peaceful protests to raise awareness of the problems faced in favelas and hundreds of children joined her on the streets. She convinced both the police and gangs to let children walk to and from school safely. In 2008 Mayra won the International Children's Peace Prize for her determination to protect Brazilian children from violence and help them access education. Mayra used the prize money to start community projects to give young people an alternative to gang culture, helping them stay safe from harm.

"Education is the key to breaking the vicious cycle of poverty and violence."

BARUANI NDUME

(BORN 1993, DEMOCRATIC REPUBLIC OF CONGO)

When children are made refugees by war or natural disaster, they are forced to flee their homes and leave everything behind: their friends, toys and school. Some find homes in a new country, while others, like Baruani Ndume, live in refugee camps. Refugee children are often alone and traumatized by their experiences. They have the right to special help but they don't always get it, or even know they have a right to it. When Baruani saw this, he worked to give his fellow child refugees a voice so that their rights were respected.

BARUANI lived with his father, mother and younger brother in a village in Congo during a time of war. Sadly, when Baruani was four his father died. But worse was yet to come.

When Baruani was seven, his house was set ablaze by rebel fighters. He escaped, but lost his family.

After many difficult days Baruani reached a refugee camp in Tanzania, but without support he struggled to survive.

For a while Baruani lived with a foster family, but he was beaten, denied food and made to work long hours.

Then, when he was nine, a teacher told Baruani that refugee children have the right to special help.

I can't imagine being a refugee, Dot.

Nearly 50 million children are refugees.

That number's too big to imagine.

This changed Baruani's life. He decided to help other refugee children to voice their needs and share their stories.

With very basic equipment, Baruani started a radio programme, "Sisi kwa Sisi" (Children for Children). Now the children could speak to a big audience.

The programme was such a success that it was aired on national radio in Tanzania, Congo, Rwanda and Burundi, helping to raise awareness of the children's concerns. Most importantly, it even helped reunite families that had been separated in the chaos of war. In 2009, Baruani was awarded the International Children's Peace Prize. His belief that everyone can make a difference and determination to give every child a voice helped many refugee children to look towards a brighter future!

"We are refugees, we are children, we are human beings."

Baruani did a good thing.

His mum would be really proud of him.

He's a life changer!

KESZ VALDEZ
(BORN 1998, PHILIPPINES)

Sometimes it isn't possible for a child to live with their birth family. Some parents are too poor or in such difficult circumstances that they can't care for a child. When this happens and a child has to be fostered or adopted, they have a right to special help and protection. Without this, children can be very vulnerable and even end up living on the streets, as happened to Kesz Valdez. After many difficult years Kesz got the help he needed, but he never forgot the children who were not so lucky.

KESZ was born into a very poor family in Cavite City. Soon after his birth, Kesz's parents tried to sell him because they couldn't afford another mouth to feed. But nobody wanted baby Kesz. So when Kesz turned two they sent him out to beg.

Kesz was hardly more than a toddler, but if he failed to bring home enough money he was beaten.

Finally, Kesz ran away – he was only four years old. With nowhere to go he lived on the streets.

For the next two years, Kesz joined many other street children scavenging on the city dump.

One day, Kesz fell onto some flaming tyres and was badly burned. He spent a long time in hospital.

This is my favourite right!

Everyone should have a home.

Lucky Kesz finding Mr Harnin.

MICHAELA MYCROFT

(BORN 1994, SOUTH AFRICA)

Millions of children face extra mental or physical challenges because of a disability. These children have the right to special help so that they can take part in life to the full and enjoy all their other rights. It is often not a disability that holds a child back, but the attitude of others, their environment or, like Michaela Mycroft, just not having the right wheelchair. Inspired by the difference the right help made to her life, Michaela supported other disabled children across South Africa.

MICHAELA, known as "Chaeli" to her friends, was born with cerebral palsy, which limited the function of her arms and her legs but not her ambition. She was determined to keep up with her friends – only sometimes the person pushing her wheelchair just wasn't fast enough!

When Chaeli was nine, her sister Erin and their friends began to raise funds for an expensive, super fast, motorized wheelchair. They made and sold cards, cookies and flower pots.

Incredibly, in seven weeks they earned enough money for the wheelchair that helped Chaeli to keep up with her friends! She decided that every child with a disability deserved the same chance.

Hooray for Chaeli and Erin!

And their friends, Tarryn, Justine and Chelsea!

They are five star heroes!

So Chaeli and the girls continued fundraising to help other children. "The Chaeli Campaign" quickly grew and began to change the lives of hundreds of children with disabilities who might otherwise have missed out on opportunities.

In 2011, Chaeli won the International Children's Peace Prize for her support of young people who face extra difficulties in life. But Chaeli didn't stop there. She continued to raise money for The Chaeli Campaign by taking part in sponsored challenges. In 2015, she became the first female without the full use of her arms and legs to reach the summit of Mount Kilimanjaro, the highest mountain in Africa. Chaeli celebrated her twenty-first birthday on top of the mountain! Chaeli's incredible achievements have shown what children with disabilities can do when they are given the special help that they deserve.

"I can tell you from experience that a child's power is no less in a differently abled body."

KEHKASHAN BASU

(BORN 2000, UNITED ARAB EMIRATES)

Every child deserves to live a healthy life in a safe environment. But sadly, millions of children die every year from illnesses that could have been prevented. Sometimes this is because families can't get good healthcare or don't have the information they need to keep themselves well. But often, as Kehkashan Basu discovered, poor health is caused by problems with the environment like dirty water and pollution. So Kehkashan decided to get as many young people as she could to fight for a healthier planet for children everywhere.

KEHKASHAN was born in Dubai on 5th June, World Environment Day. From an early age she loved visiting her grandmother's garden and was passionate about all of nature. Her favourite animal was the koala!

This is literally the cutest animal I've ever seen.

Time to take action!

One day, Kehkashan was shocked to see a picture of a bird killed by eating plastic. She decided it was time to act to look after the environment.

We can't let our birds and planet die!

Kehkashan and her friends began to collect and recycle litter. Then, on her eighth birthday, she planted her first tree.

What are we?

We are the future – we are the change!

But Kehkashan wanted to get more young people involved, so when she was twelve she founded Green Hope, a movement of passionate youth fighting to protect our planet.

Every year over a million children die due to pollution.

Every day trees are cut down and animals are trapped in plastic.

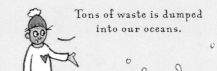
Tons of waste is dumped into our oceans.

Kehkashan inspired over a thousand volunteers from lots of different countries to join Green Hope. They raised awareness of environmental issues, organized recycling operations, cleaned up beaches and planted trees all across the globe. Kehkashan also organized events to encourage other young people to care for the environment. In 2016 Kehkashan won the International Children's Peace Prize for her outstanding efforts to make our planet healthier and more sustainable – a place where all children can enjoy their right to a safe and healthy life.

"Take that extra step, walk that extra mile to get the future we want."

So let's be the change and plant trees.

Let's recycle our waste and be litter pickers.

Kehkashan believed every child can help – and we can!

RYAN HRELJAC

(BORN 1991, CANADA)

Most children enjoy their right to food, clean water, clothing and a place to live – Ryan Hreljac did! So he was shocked to learn that some children live on the streets or in homes that don't provide what they need, making it hard for them to enjoy their other rights. Ryan was particularly upset to hear that some children have to walk for miles every day to collect water. Sometimes, this journey takes so long that the children have no time for school. Ryan was only six years old when he learned this, but he was determined to help.

RYAN grew up in Canada. One day, while he was at primary school, Ryan learned that in parts of Africa children have to walk so far to fetch water that they miss out on school. Worse still, the water they collect often carries disease that makes them sick.

Even little children.

All I do is turn a tap!

Ryan was so upset, he started to do extra household chores to raise the money to dig a well for a village in northern Uganda.

Now off to school.

Our well!

Eventually, through hard work and donations, Ryan raised enough money for a well. It was built next to a school in the Oyam District of Uganda.

Jimmy Akana, a boy from the school, became Ryan's pen pal. Jimmy's parents had disappeared during the country's civil war and he was living with an aunt. Before the well was built, Jimmy had risen every night at midnight to walk eight kilometres to fetch water for his aunt before school.

Imagine not being able to turn on a tap to get a drink of water.

In my house, there are seven water taps.

Well, make sure they're not dripping.

A year later Ryan and his family went to see the well in action and visit Jimmy. The whole community came together to celebrate the difference the well had made to their lives.

On his return home, Ryan was inspired to start the Ryan's Well Foundation charity, so that he could build more wells in remote communities.

A project that started with a little boy doing household chores has since provided many thousands of people in sixteen different countries with accessible, clean water, safe toilets and washing facilities! This saves lives and gives children more time for education and fun. It also gives adults more time for work, which helps to improve the lives of the whole family. Ryan believes that everyone can make a difference and encourages others to help him raise money for his projects. As for Jimmy, he eventually moved to Canada to live with Ryan's family and help the Ryan's Well Foundation give more children the water they have the right to.

"You are never too young or too old to make a difference — just find your passion!"

MALALA YOUSAFZAI
(BORN 1997, PAKISTAN)

You may find it hard to imagine not going to school, but some children struggle to get an education. This is what happened to Malala Yousafzai when religious groups in her country wanted to stop girls going to school. Other children face different obstacles to Malala – they may live in a poor area where there are few schools, or they might have to work to help support their family. Whatever the reason, without an education it can be hard to find a job or achieve your dreams – which is why Malala fought for the right to an education.

MALALA grew up in the Swat Valley of Pakistan and went to a school started by her father, Ziauddin. Malala loved school and was devastated when the Taliban, an extreme religious group, started closing girls' schools in the area.

There's so much to learn and we want to learn it all!

"How dare the Taliban take away my basic right to education?"

Malala, then aged eleven, publicly demanded that the Taliban allowed girls an education.

The Taliban are beating people in the streets.

My father started this school, we have a right to be here.

I'm scared.

Malala, and many of her friends, continued to go to school in spite of the real danger.

Education is my favourite right.

Mine too, because I want a huge brain!

I love the right to free speech, too.

They won't hurt a girl, but what about you, Papa?

Which one of you is Malala?

Malala began to receive death threats, but she was more worried about her father, who was an anti-Taliban activist, than for herself.

But on 9th October 2012, a gunman boarded Malala's school bus. He shot Malala in the head and wounded two of her friends.

She'll be safer in England.

Your family will follow soon.

We must hurry.

Miraculously Malala survived, and when she was strong enough she was flown to England for treatment. It was a lonely journey, but her family followed as quickly as they could.

"I raise my voice not so that I can shout, but so that those without a voice can be heard."

SUCCESSFUL NATION

EDUCATION FOR ALL!

UNITE WITH MALALA!

We raise our voices with you!

UNITE WITH MALALA!

EDUCATION IS MY RIGHT

Malala recovered from her injuries and courageously continued her campaign for a child's right to an education. She was awarded the Nobel Peace Prize and the International Children's Peace Prize for her bravery and commitment. Malala's refusal to allow the Taliban to silence her inspired many other young people to speak out for their right to an education, helping to spread the message that education is the right of every child, whatever their gender and wherever they live.

"One child, one teacher, one book and one pen can change the world."

Can I say something?

You can and you may!

Ah, but will we listen – that is the question!

RILEY HEBBARD

(BORN 2005, USA)

Would you have guessed that you actually have a right to play? It might just seem like fun, but your right to relax, play and join in a wide range of activities is an important part of helping you grow into a confident adult. If you live in a wealthy country you may take this right for granted, but to children suffering from poverty, poor health or a lack of food, play may not seem as important as surviving. Riley Hebbard realized this and, as young as she was, she knew just how to help!

RILEY was only four years old when, in 2009, she saw a television programme about a Darfur refugee camp in Sudan. She was upset to see that the children had no toys and were playing with mud, stones and sticks.

She was meant to be getting ready for school, but Riley wanted to help right away, so she marched off to her room.

There Riley collected together lots of her toys and asked her mum if they could send them to the refugee children.

Later that morning Riley decided to ask her school friends if they would donate their toys too.

Word of the collection quickly spread through the local community and gifts of toys and money started to pour in!

Riley's mum spoke to World Vision, a charity that supports vulnerable children, to ask if they would deliver the toys.

World Vision agreed and each time Riley and her friends had collected enough donations, World Vision sent them to the areas that needed them most. Not only do the toys bring a smile to the faces of children, but they give them the chance to stretch their imaginations, learn new skills and do better at school! Thousands of children throughout the world have received toys and games from Riley's Toys Foundation, helping them to realize their right to relax and play.

"Whenever I'm helping I don't want to stop, because it makes me really happy!"

IQBAL MASIH
(BORN 1983, PAKISTAN)

You may not be able to imagine being sent out to work at four years old, but that is what happened to Iqbal Masih and thousands of other children like him. Every child has the right to protection from labour that damages their health, education and their other rights. But Iqbal, like many others, didn't know this and struggled to escape from his difficult and dangerous work. Eventually Iqbal learned of his rights and he began to campaign to raise awareness among other children and protect them from forced labour.

IQBAL was born into a poor family in the city of Muridke, Pakistan. His family found it almost impossible to survive and often went hungry. When Iqbal was four, his family borrowed money from the owner of a carpet business.

We have no food, just bills.

Give me the boy and I'll give you money.

You're mine now!

To pay off the debt, little Iqbal had to go and work for the carpet maker. Iqbal worked from dawn to dusk every day.

Keep working or he'll beat you.

You'll never pay off the interest on your debts.

Along with other children, Iqbal was chained to the loom tying knots in wool to make carpets, but his family's debt never decreased.

This is a most excellent right.

Can you imagine being chained to anything?

I wouldn't even chain up a dog.

When Iqbal was ten years old, he escaped. He was very scared.

Unfortunately he was caught by the police and was returned to the factory.

But Iqbal was desperate, and finally he managed to escape again.

This time he was taken in by a school run by the Bonded Labour Liberation Front. To keep him small enough to work on the loom, Iqbal had been underfed, so he was tiny for his age. But his brain worked brilliantly and he finished a four year school course in two years!

Iqbal was determined to help other children forced to work against their will. He gave talks, marched and campaigned to end child labour all over the world, and helped free over 3,000 Pakistani children working to pay off debts. Iqbal hoped to become a lawyer so that he could help even more children, but in 1995 he was murdered. It is not known who murdered him, but despite his tragic death Iqbal remains a shining symbol of the fight against child labour. His bravery continues to inspire others.

"Children should have pens in their hands, not tools!"

Iqbal was very brave.

He never gave up.

He is my super, superhero!

EMMANUEL JAL

(BORN 1980, SUDAN)

If you live in a peaceful country, it might be hard to believe there are hundreds of thousands of children as young as eight who are forced to fight in wars across the world. Emmanuel Jal was one of them – he was made to join the army in Sudan. Other child soldiers fight to defend their community, and some are just hoping to be fed. Children have a right to protection from the horrors and trauma of war, so Emmanuel used his own experiences to stand up for this right.

EMMANUEL grew up in Sudan during a time of civil war. His father joined the Sudan People's Liberation Army (SPLA), but when Emmanuel was seven years old, his mother was killed and he was captured by the same soldiers.

Don't worry, we will look after you.

Will we be fed?

We'll see you get an education.

Emmanuel and a group of other children were taken to Ethiopia and promised an education.

We have to escape.

Keep fighting or they'll kill us!

Instead the children were trained as soldiers and forced to fight for the SPLA in the civil war.

We were over three hundred and now we are sixteen.

Quiet, just keep walking.

After five years, Emmanuel made a dangerous escape from the soldiers' camp with a group of other children. It took them three months of walking to escape, and many died on the journey without food or water.

Adults shouldn't start wars.

Try telling them that, Lou.

War is the thief of childhood and family.

Eventually, Emmanuel was rescued by Emma McCune, an aid worker, who adopted him and smuggled him to Nairobi, Kenya.

Sadly, Emma died shortly afterwards and Emmanuel struggled to finish his education while living in the slums of Nairobi.

Then Emmanuel discovered hip-hop music and started to sing to relieve the pain of his life.

He also began to raise money for local street children and refugees.

After finishing his education in England, Emmanuel became a rapper, using the power of music to tell his story and campaign against violence and the use of child soldiers. Emmanuel founded a charity, Gua Africa, to offer scholarships to refugees and former child soldiers and fund their teachers and school supplies. Gua means peace in Emmanuel's native Nuer language. The charity also campaigns for global peace and helps to rescue child soldiers who, like Emmanuel, have had their right to a childhood taken away.

"My childhood was stolen."

MORE WORLD CHANGERS

The activists in this book are not the only ones who have done amazing things to fight for your rights. All over the world there are people supporting children's rights. And it's not just children – there are lots of brilliant adult activists too! But there's always more work to be done and we can all help. You have the right to be listened to by adults, and using your voice is an important way to raise awareness of children's rights. When adults know about your rights and listen to your opinions, they can help you make a difference. No matter how young you are, YOU can be a world changer – as these activists show!

"Translate empathy into action."

NEHA GUPTA, USA

Neha founded Empower Orphans to help orphans and abandoned children across the world. In 2014 Neha was awarded the International Children's Peace Prize.

OM PRAKASH GURJAR, India

Om Prakash was forced into work at the age of five. He finally escaped and started to campaign against child labour. He was awarded the International Children's Peace Prize in 2006.

"I want to help the little people."

"Include us, have us as friends, fight for our place at school. I am capable of more than you think, because in my heart I am strong."

"I think it is a good idea to help children who do not have the support some of us have."

OSCAR ANDERSON, UK

Oscar speaks up for the rights of all young people with disabilities. He also campaigned for babies all over the world to be tested for jaundice, an illness which in very rare cases can cause brain damage.

ISRAELI TARWAY, Liberia

At the age of seven Israeli started to save half her lunch money, and walk around with a charity box, to raise money to send underprivileged children to school. She won the Diana Award for young people in 2017.

Can I be an activist?

Of course – every child can.

Am I every child?

"We've learned that kids can do things. We can make things happen!"

MELATI AND ISABEL WIJSEN, Bali

In 2013, sisters Melati and Isabel, then ten and twelve years old, started a campaign to reduce plastic waste and stop the use of plastic bags in Bali.

"School is power, school is everything."

MUZOON ALMELLEHAN, Syria

Muzoon fled to Jordan from war-torn Syria when she was fourteen. She campaigned for refugee children's right to an education and became UNICEF's youngest Goodwill Ambassador.

"All violence against children is preventable."

ABRAHAM M. KEITA, Liberia

Abraham campaigned against child violence in his community and for laws on child rights. In 2015 he was awarded the International Children's Peace Prize.

"I just know we must prioritize lives over guns."
Dylan Redshaw

MARJORY STONEMAN DOUGLAS STUDENTS, USA

In 2018, seventeen people were murdered in a shooting at a school in Florida. Student survivors campaigned against school and gun violence with rallies and protests across America. A group of the students won the 2018 International Children's Peace Prize.

HILARY ELLIOT DOGBE, Ghana

Prompted by violence in his community, Hilary started peace marches that eventually involved over 15,000 children. In 2017 he became his country's Peace Ambassador.

"We must cherish and protect peace for the sake of children."

THANDIWE CHAMA, Zambia

When Thandiwe was eight her school closed, so she led her classmates on a walk to find a new school. In 2007, Thandiwe was awarded the International Children's Peace Prize for her continued campaign for education.

"I believe that all children should go to school."

"Education consists of a traffic of knowledge and experiences."

AMELIA SALAMÉ, Chile

Born as a boy, Amelia was discriminated against at school for her long hair and make-up. She became an activist to raise awareness of the injustices suffered by LGBT children, especially in rural areas.

Yes, and more!

We can be more, because of these children.

Thank you activists, every one!

KNOW YOUR RIGHTS!

The UN Convention on the Rights of the Child has 54 articles and 196 countries have agreed to follow them. All the rights are equally important. They aim to do what is best for you as long as it's not harmful to others. The original list was written for governments and international organizations to understand – this is a simpler version. Remember these are YOUR rights! Once you know them you can stand up for them, for yourself and for others!

ARTICLE 1 Everyone under eighteen has these rights.

ARTICLE 2 You have these rights no matter who you are or what your race, sex or religion is.

ARTICLE 3 Adults should always do what is best for you.

ARTICLE 4 The government should protect your rights.

ARTICLE 5 Your parents or family should help you to benefit from your rights.

ARTICLE 6 You have the right to be alive.

ARTICLE 7 You have the right to a name and a nationality.

ARTICLE 8 You have the right to an identity (an official record of who you are).

ARTICLE 9 You have the right to live with your parents, unless it is harmful for you to do so.

ARTICLE 10 If your parents are in another country you have the right to be reunited with them.

ARTICLE 11 You should not be taken out of your country illegally.

ARTICLE 12 You have the right to an opinion, to be listened to and taken seriously.

ARTICLE 13 You have the right to find things out and share your ideas, unless they harm others.

ARTICLE 14 You can choose your own religion and beliefs, with the help of your parents.

ARTICLE 15 You have the right to choose your own friends and form groups and clubs.

ARTICLE 16 You have the right to privacy.

ARTICLE 17 You have the right to information that is helpful and not harmful through TV, books and elsewhere.

ARTICLE 18 You have the right to be raised by your parents, if that is possible.

ARTICLE 19 You have the right to protection from being mentally or physically harmed.

ARTICLE 20 You have the right to special care if you can't live with your parents.

ARTICLE 21 You have the right to the best possible care if you are adopted or in foster care.

ARTICLE 22 You have the right to special care and protection if you are a refugee.

ARTICLE 23 If you have a disability you have the right to help so you can live a full life.

ARTICLE 24 You have the right to good healthcare and a safe environment.

ARTICLE 25 If you live in care your living arrangements should be regularly checked.

ARTICLE 26 You have the right to help from the government if you are poor or in need.

ARTICLE 27 You have the right to food, clothing and a safe place to live with your basic needs met.

ARTICLE 28 You have the right to the best possible education.

ARTICLE 29 Your education should develop your talents and teach you to respect others.

ARTICLE 30 You have the right to practise your own language, culture and religion.

ARTICLE 31 You have the right to play and relax.

Let's learn our rights together!

I will, if you will?

That's what together is, silly.

ARTICLE 32 You have the right to protection from work that harms you or your education.

ARTICLE 33 You have the right to be protected from dangerous drugs.

ARTICLE 34 You have the right to protection from sexual abuse.

ARTICLE 35 No one is allowed to kidnap or sell you.

ARTICLE 36 No one should take advantage of you.

ARTICLE 37 You should not be punished in a cruel or harmful way.

ARTICLE 38 You have the right to protection from war. Children under fifteen cannot be forced to join the army.

ARTICLE 39 You have the right to help if you have been hurt, neglected or ill-treated.

ARTICLE 40 If you break the law or are accused of a crime you have the right to legal help and a fair trial.

ARTICLE 41 If your country has any better rights than these, you have a right to them.

ARTICLE 42 You have a right to know your rights, and adults should also know them.

ARTICLES 43–54 These rights are about how governments and international organizations will work to support children's rights.

INTERNATIONAL CHILDREN'S RIGHTS ORGANIZATIONS

There are lots of organizations all over the world that support and protect your rights. These are just a few of them.

UNICEF (United Nations Children's Fund)
Founded in 1946 to help protect children after World War Two, the Rights of the Child is the basis of all of UNICEF's work. It also provides emergency supplies and support in times of crisis.

KidsRights Foundation
Founded in 2003 and based in the Netherlands, KidsRights raises funds for aid projects around the world, to support and empower vulnerable children. It aims above all to make sure children's voices are heard.

Save the Children
Founded in 1919 by sisters Eglantyne Jebb and Dorothy Buxton, Save the Children promotes children's rights and provides relief and support for children in developing countries. Its mission is to fight for children's rights and help them fulfil their potential.

Defence for Children International
Founded in 1979 during the first International Year of the Child, this organization is based in Switzerland. It works with groups all over the world to protect children's rights.

"Humanity owes the child the best it has to give."

Eglantyne Jebb and Dorothy Buxton

 If you're under eighteen ...

YOU have these rights!

Three hoots
for them!

INDEX

**Wherever you see speech marks in this book,
it means that's a real quote. How many inspiring
quotes from these amazing activists can you find?**

We are
the future.

We are
the change!